W9-AVW-599

Presented to:

_____

Presented by:

_____

Date:

_____

THE BEGINNERS BIBLE

Bedtime Stories and Prayers

™

Unless otherwise indicated, all Scripture quotations and references are taken from the New Revised Standard Version of the Bible NRSV copyright © 1989 by The Division of Christian Education of the National Council of the Churches of Christ in the USA. Used by permission. All rights reserved.

The Beginners Bible—Bedtime Stories and Prayers
ISBN 1-56292-939-9
Artwork/Text: Copyright © 2000 by James R. Leininger. The Beginners Bible trademarks and copyrights are owned by James R. Leininger and licensed exclusively to Performance Unlimited, Inc., Brentwood, Tennessee.
All rights reserved.

Published by Honor Books
P. O. Box 55388
Tulsa, Oklahoma 74155

Printed in the United States of America. All rights reserved under International Copyright Law. Contents and/or cover may not be reproduced in whole or in part in any form without the express written consent of the Publisher.

Introduction

How many times have you said, "Read me a story!" Probably a lot! One of the best books to read at bedtime is the Bible. It's full of amazing adventures and super stories about God and His people . . . like the time Moses parted the Red Sea so the children of Israel could escape the Egyptian army . . . or when King Saul threw a spear at David . . . or when brave Queen Esther saved her people. Then there are the wonderful stories about Jesus . . . like the time when he was twelve years old and his parents couldn't find him . . . or how he healed people of terrible diseases . . . or how he stopped a storm.

Just reading about how much God loves you and how he takes care of his people makes you feel safe. It makes you want to say, "Thank you, God, for loving me!" We've included a prayer at the end of each story for you to say at bedtime. The prayers will help you talk to God.

So hop into bed, snuggle up against your pillow, and read God's *Bedtime Stories and Prayers*. Sweet dreams!

Table of Contents

Noah Builds an Ark

Genesis 6:9

● ●

Long ago, most of the people in the world did not love God. They were not kind to each other. God searched the world to find one good person. He found a man named Noah. Noah and his family loved God and worshiped him.

God told Noah that he was going to flood the earth, but Noah and his family would be safe. God gave Noah instructions for building a big boat called an ark.

Noah trusted God. He listened to God. Noah began building the ark right away. His wife, his three sons, and his sons' wives helped build it, too.

They used a special kind of wood that would help the big boat float. They built the ark exactly the way God had planned. Noah and his family worked on the ark for a long time. Finally, the big boat was finished.

God sent Noah two of every animal in the world. Noah and his family loaded the animals onto the ark. They also filled the ark with lots of food and supplies.

Then God sent rain. The rain fell for many days. When the rain stopped, the flood covered everything. But Noah, his family, and the animals were safe.

Dear God,

I know you care for me. You care for my family, too. You watch over me and keep me safe all day long. Thank you for keeping me safe while I am asleep at night. Please keep my friends safe, too.

Amen

Abraham's Guests

Genesis 18:1

● ●

Abraham and his wife, Sarah, loved God. They owned many sheep and other animals. They traveled to different places to find grass for their flocks. They lived in a tent that they carried with them.

One hot day, Abraham was sitting in front of their tent. Three strangers walked up to him. They had been sent by God to give him a special message. But Abraham thought they were just hungry travelers.

Abraham quickly stood up and greeted the men. He gave them cool water to drink. He even offered to wash their feet. While the men rested under a tree, Abraham and his family prepared a meal for them.

Sarah made fresh bread. Their helper cooked some meat. Abraham brought them milk and other food.

Then one of the visitors told Abraham that Sarah

would have a baby boy. Sarah heard what the man said. She laughed because she believed that she was too old to have a child.

Abraham said goodbye to the strange visitors. Later Sarah did have a baby boy. His name was Isaac. God had performed a miracle for them!

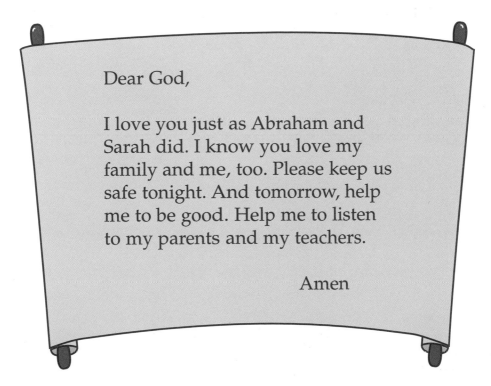

Dear God,

I love you just as Abraham and Sarah did. I know you love my family and me, too. Please keep us safe tonight. And tomorrow, help me to be good. Help me to listen to my parents and my teachers.

Amen

Jacob Has a Dream

Genesis 28:10-11

● ●

Isaac and his wife, Rebekah, had twin sons. Esau was their oldest son, and Jacob was their youngest. Esau was jealous of Jacob because Jacob was Rebekah's favorite son.

The two sons lived with their parents even after they grew up. Now Isaac was very old. Soon Esau would become the leader of the family.

But Jacob tricked his father into making him the leader of their family. This made Esau so angry that he wanted to kill Jacob. So Jacob ran away from home.

Jacob traveled far away. One night, he stopped to rest. He found a rock and used it for his pillow. During the night, Jacob had a strange dream.

A long stairway reached from the ground all the way up to heaven. Angels from heaven were walking up

and down the stairs. Then God spoke to Jacob in his dream. Someday, the place where he was sleeping would belong to his family. God also promised to watch over him. Jacob thanked God for guiding him to this special place.

The next morning, Jacob prayed to God. He promised to love God and obey him.

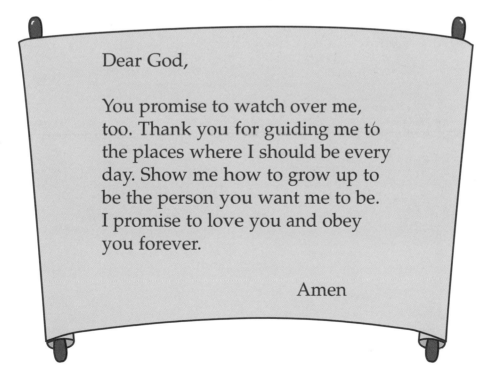

Dear God,

You promise to watch over me, too. Thank you for guiding me to the places where I should be every day. Show me how to grow up to be the person you want me to be. I promise to love you and obey you forever.

Amen

Baby Moses Is Saved

Exodus 2:1-2

● ●

Egypt's new ruler did not like the Israelites who lived in Egypt. He was cruel to them. He forced them to work very hard for him every day. They made bricks from mud for Pharaoh's buildings. They also built cities for Pharaoh and his people.

After many years, Pharaoh decided that there were too many Israelites in Egypt. He ordered his soldiers to get rid of the Israelite baby boys born in Egypt.

One woman had a plan to save her son. She found a basket and covered it with tar so that it would float. She placed her baby in the basket and put it in the river. Her daughter followed the basket as it floated away.

Pharaoh's daughter walked down to the river with her servants. She saw the basket floating by. She found the baby and wanted to keep him at the palace. She

named him Moses. Then Moses' sister had an idea. She told Pharaoh's daughter that she knew a woman who would care for the baby until he was older. The woman was Moses' own mother!

Pharaoh's daughter agreed. Moses' mother cared for him for many years. Then she returned him to the palace to live with Pharaoh's daughter.

Dear God,

Just like Moses, you knew me when I was a tiny baby. You had a plan for my life even then. You knew my name, and you knew my family. Thank you that you will always love me. Please watch over me and keep me safe.

Amen

Lots of Frogs

Exodus 8:1

• •

For a long time, many Israelites lived peacefully in Egypt. Then a new ruler came into power. He made the Israelites work as his slaves.

God sent Moses to Egypt to free his people. Moses and his brother, Aaron, went to Pharaoh's palace. Moses told Pharaoh to let his people go.

But Pharaoh did not believe in God. He was not afraid of God's power. Pharaoh would not let the Israelites go. So God sent a plague to Egypt to show his power to Pharaoh.

In the first plague, God made all the water turn to blood. But Pharaoh still would not let the Israelites go. So God sent another plague. He told Moses to have Aaron wave his walking stick in the air. The rivers and streams were filled with frogs. There were frogs

hopping everywhere. Pharaoh's servants could not keep them away from the palace. Frogs were even hopping in the kitchen and bedrooms.

Pharaoh agreed to set the Israelites free. But when God sent the frogs away, Pharaoh refused to let them go. After eight more plagues, Pharaoh finally gave the Israelites their freedom.

Dear God,

You are so powerful! Yet you are so full of love and kindness. Pharaoh should have listened to you. Thank you that I am one of your children. Thank you that you will always love me. Please help me to always listen to you and do what's right.

Amen

Moses Parts the Red Sea

Exodus 14:1-2

● ●

With God's help, Moses led the Israelites out of Egypt. Pharaoh had finally set them free. Now God was going to lead them to their new home in the promised land of Canaan.

Soon after the Israelites left Egypt, Pharaoh changed his mind. He ordered his soldiers to help him find the Israelites and bring them back to Egypt.

Moses and the Israelites stopped to rest near the Red Sea. They saw Pharaoh and his troops coming toward them. The Israelites lost their faith in God. They were frightened that Pharaoh and his soldiers would kill them all.

But Moses trusted God. He knew that God would save them from Pharaoh's army. Moses walked to the edge of the sea. He held his hand over the water. With

God's help, the sea parted and made a path to the other side. Moses and the Israelites crossed safely across the path. But when Pharaoh's soldiers tried to cross the path, the sea spilled down on top of them.

Now the Israelites were truly free to begin their long journey to Canaan. They sang and praised God for saving them from Pharaoh's army.

Dear God,

I trust you, too! I know you're always there to lead me. When I get into trouble, I know you'll help me. Thank you for protecting me. Help me to remember all the good things you do for me.

Amen

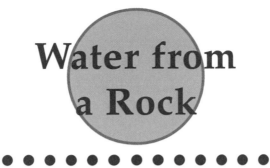

Water from a Rock

Exodus 17:1

● ●

After leaving Egypt, Moses and the Israelites began the long journey to the land that God had promised them. There would be plenty of food and water in their new home. Their animals would have lots of green grass to eat. But they had to travel through the wilderness to get there.

The wilderness was mostly hot and dry. Soon the people began to run out of food and water. They did not trust God to help them. They told Moses that they should have never left Egypt. At least they had plenty of food and water when they were slaves.

So God sent them sweet bread from heaven called *manna*. Every morning, the ground was covered with manna. There was always enough for everyone.

Later the Israelites camped in an area where there

was no water. They became angry with Moses again. Moses prayed to God for help.

God led Moses and other leaders from the group to a big rock. Moses hit the rock with his walking stick. Water poured out of the rock. When the rest of the group arrived, there was plenty of water for them and their animals.

Dear God,

You have given me such good promises in the Bible. Thank you for your promise to take care of my family and me. Keep me from grumbling and complaining when things don't go my way. And please remind me to pray when I need your help.

Amen

Balaam's Donkey Speaks

Numbers 22:23

● ●

The king of Moab did not like the Israelites. He sent his helpers to find a prophet named Balaam. The king wanted Balaam to place a curse on the Israelites. The king hoped that the curse would cause bad things to happen to them.

The king's helpers found Balaam. He agreed to see the king. Balaam climbed onto his donkey and headed toward the palace.

Suddenly the donkey saw an angel from heaven blocking the road. So the donkey left the road. Balaam did not see the angel. He became angry and struck the donkey. He made the donkey return to the road.

Two more times, the angel blocked them from going down the road. Each time, the donkey saw the angel and stopped. But Balaam did not see the angel. He

struck the donkey each time. Finally, the angel allowed the donkey to speak. The donkey asked Balaam to stop hitting him. Then Balaam saw the angel.

Balaam was sorry for striking his donkey. The angel told him to see the king. But he must bless the Israelites instead of placing a curse on them. Balaam blessed the Israelites.

Dear God,

Sometimes I get angry with other people, and I say mean things. I'm sorry. Help me to be a better person. I want to be kind and loving. Help me to be nice to my family and friends. Thank you that you are helping me to bless them.

Amen

Joshua's Two Spies

Joshua 2:1

● ●

After Moses died, Joshua led the Israelites to the promised land of Canaan. When they reached Canaan, they found a city surrounded by big walls. It was the city of Jericho.

Joshua knew that Jericho's king would never let the Israelites live peacefully in Canaan. So Joshua sent two brave men to spy on Jericho's army.

The two spies moved quietly through Jericho. They did not want to get caught by the king's soldiers. They met a woman named Rahab and told her why they were there. She agreed to help them if they would not harm her family. The two men agreed.

The king found out that the spies had entered the city. He sent some of his soldiers to find them. The soldiers went from house to house, searching for the

two spies. So Rahab hid the two men on the roof of her house. When the soldiers asked her about the spies, she said that she had seen them, but now they were gone.

The soldiers believed Rahab and went away. Then Rahab helped the two spies escape. She lowered a long rope from her window. Then the two men climbed down the rope and returned to camp.

Dear God,

The spies who went into Jericho were so brave! I want to be brave, too. I want to let other people know how good you are. Help me know when it's safe to tell others about you. But most of all, help me to show people your love.

Amen

The Walls of Jericho

Joshua 6:1

● ●

Joshua and the Israelites had finally reached the land of Canaan. They wanted to live peacefully in their new home.

As the Israelites traveled through Canaan, they came upon the city of Jericho. The king of Jericho did not want the Israelites in Canaan. Joshua's army would have to defeat the king's soldiers before the Israelites could live in peace.

God was watching over the Israelites. Before the big battle, God told Joshua how his army could defeat the king's soldiers. Joshua and his men did exactly what God told them to do.

First, Joshua and his men marched once around the high walls surrounding the city. Seven priests blew their trumpets. They all did the same thing each day for

six days. On the seventh day, they marched around the city seven times. The priests blew their trumpets. The rest of Joshua's men shouted.

The walls around the city tumbled to the ground! Joshua led his men into the city, and they defeated the king's soldiers. By listening to God, Joshua's army won the battle.

Dear God,

Even though I'm just a kid, sometimes I face big problems in my life, too. Thank you that you are always there to fight for me. I don't have to face my problems alone. Help me to put your plan into action. I know that when I do, I will win!

Amen

God Calls Gideon

Judges 6:36-37

● ●

For many years, the Israelites did not have an army to help them fight their enemies. Whenever they tried to grow food to eat, their enemies would destroy their crops.

So God sent an angel to give a message to a man named Gideon. The angel watched Gideon as he worked. Gideon was hiding food from his enemies. The angel told Gideon that God had chosen him to lead the Israelites into battle against their enemies.

Gideon did not believe that he was the right man for the job. Gideon wanted a sign from God that he would help the Israelites defeat their enemies. Gideon placed a pile of wool on the ground. He told God that he would leave the wool there until the next morning. If the wool was wet and the ground was dry, he would know that

God would help the Israelites.

The next morning, the wool was wet and the ground was dry. Then Gideon asked for another sign from God. Finally, Gideon knew that God would help him and the Israelites. With God's help, he would lead the Israelites in chasing away their enemies.

Dear God,

Thank you that your angels watch over my family and me. I can't see them, but I know you have asked them to keep me safe. When I don't know what to do, guide me to make the right decision. Thank you for making me wise.

Amen

Gideon's Victory

Judges 7:1

● ●

The Israelites did not have an army to save them from an enemy army. So they prayed to God for help. God chose a farmer named Gideon to help them. Gideon did not know anything about leading an army. But he loved God and listened to him.

Gideon gathered a large army to fight the enemy soldiers. But God told Gideon that he did not need a large army to win. So Gideon told his soldiers that if any of them were afraid to fight, they could go home.

Many of his soldiers went home. Then Gideon took the rest of his men down to the river to drink some water. Some soldiers scooped up the water and drank it from their hands. Others lowered their heads and drank from the river. The ones who drank from their hands were chosen to follow Gideon into battle.

Gideon led his small group to the enemy camp. They carried torches, clay jars, and horns. When Gideon blew his horn, his soldiers smashed their clay jars on the ground. Then they blew their horns and shouted. The enemy soldiers were frightened by the noise and ran away. God had helped Gideon's army defeat their enemies without a fight.

Dear God,

I love you, too! And I want to listen to you better. Thank you that when I don't know how to do something, you can help me do it. Help me to hear you and obey you just as Gideon did.

Amen

Samson
Fights a Lion

Judges 14:5

● ●

An Israelite woman and her husband never had any children. An angel appeared to them one day. The angel told them that God was going to bless them. They would have a son. The boy would grow up to be very strong. And he would be a great warrior for the Israelites.

But the angel warned them to never cut the child's hair. If their son ever cut his hair, God would take away his strength.

Just as the angel had promised, the couple had a son. His name was Samson. They allowed their son's hair to grow long. Samson wore his long hair in braids.

When Samson became a man, he was tall and very strong, just as God had promised. He fell in love with a beautiful woman and wanted to marry her. One day,

Samson and his parents went on a trip to see her. Suddenly, a big lion attacked him. But Samson was so strong that he fought the lion with his bare hands and killed it.

Then Samson and his parents continued their journey. Samson met with the woman he loved. Later, he married her.

Dear God,

I want to be strong. I want to do great things for you, too. But most of all, I want to do what you want me to do with my life. Even if I'm not strong in my body, I know you can help me be strong in my spirit. Thank you for that!

Amen

Samson Defeats an Army

Judges 15:16

● ●

For many years, the Philistines ruled over the Israelites. They forced the Israelites to work for them. The Philistines had a powerful army. Samson fought against their army so that the Israelites would be free. He defeated many soldiers. But they could never kill Samson because God made him very strong.

One day, the Philistine army attacked the people of Judah. The people asked the soldiers why they had come to Judah. The soldiers told them that they were searching for Samson.

Judah's people were afraid of the Philistine army. So they sent a group of men to talk to Samson. They told him that they were going to tie him up and hand him over to the Philistines. Samson allowed them to tie him up as long as they did not try to kill him.

Some men from Judah took Samson to the Philistine camp. The soldiers were happy to see Samson tied with ropes. Suddenly, Samson used his strength to break the ropes. He saw the jawbone of a donkey on the ground. Samson grabbed the jawbone and, with God's help, he defeated all the soldiers.

Dear God,

Thank you that I live in a free country! Help me to trust that you will keep us safe here. I pray that if I'm ever in trouble, you will give me the strength to defeat my enemies. And I pray that you will give me the tools I need to win.

Amen

Ruth and Naomi

● ●

Naomi and her husband lived in Moab with their grown sons. One son married a woman named Orpah. The other son married a woman named Ruth.

Later, Naomi's husband and two sons died. Naomi, Ruth, and Orpah were very sad. Naomi decided to move back to her old home in Bethlehem. She told Orpah and Ruth to return to their families.

Orpah and Ruth loved Naomi very much. But Orpah obeyed Naomi and returned to her family. Ruth refused to leave Naomi. Ruth knew that it would not be easy for Naomi to live alone. Ruth said, "Your people shall be my people, and your God my God."

So Naomi agreed to let Ruth stay with her. They packed up their belongings and made the long journey to Bethlehem.

Ruth went to a field every day and gathered grain. They used the grain to make flour for bread.

One day, Ruth met the man who owned the field. His name was Boaz. Ruth and Boaz became good friends. Later Ruth married Boaz. They cared for Naomi together. Ruth and Naomi were happy again.

Dear God,

I'm glad that I am a part of your family. I'm happy that I can talk to you when I pray. I can tell you anything. You know everything about me. I pray that when you ask me to follow you, I will go. Thank you for making me so happy!

Amen

Hannah's Prayer

1 Samuel 1:1-2

● ●

Hannah was married to a good man who loved her very much. But Hannah was very sad. She was not able to have any children. After a while, she became so sad that she often cried and would not eat. Her husband became very worried about her.

Hannah and her husband went to the temple to worship God. Hannah found a quiet place in the temple where she could pray. She asked God to bless her with a son. If he did, she would raise her child to worship him. She would even let her child grow up to serve God at the temple.

As Hannah prayed, she began to cry. A priest named Eli was sitting nearby. He saw Hannah and walked over to see what was wrong with her.

Hannah told Eli that she had been very sad for a

long time. She was praying to God for help. Eli told Hannah to go home. God would answer her prayers.

Hannah was not sad anymore. The next morning, Hannah and her husband returned to the temple to pray. Then they went home. Later, God blessed Hannah with a son. His name was Samuel. God had answered her prayers.

Dear God,

Thank you for hearing my prayers. I can ask you for help when I'm sad. And I can tell you when I'm happy! Thank you that you never get impatient with me. You always listen. Help me to be just as patient with other people, too.

Amen

Samuel Moves Away

1 Samuel 2:21

• •

Hannah had made a promise to God. If God blessed her with a son, she would allow her son to be raised by the priests at the temple.

God heard Hannah's prayers. God blessed Hannah and her husband with a beautiful son. Hannah named him Samuel.

Hannah kept her promise. She went to see Eli, the high priest at the temple. She asked him if he would care for her son and teach him to serve God. Eli agreed to raise and teach Samuel when the child was older.

So Hannah cared for Samuel while he was a baby. Then when Samuel was old enough, Hannah took him to the temple to stay with Eli.

Samuel became Eli's helper and student. Samuel worked and lived at the temple. Eli also taught Samuel

many things about serving God.

Even when Samuel was young, God knew he was special. God often spoke to him. When Samuel became a man, he was one of God's most faithful prophets. He taught people about God's love. When Samuel was very old, God chose him for a very important job. Samuel anointed the first king of Israel.

Dear God,

Thank you that you always keep your promises. I want to be just like you. I want to keep the promises I make to my friends and family. Help me to always tell the truth. I pray that I will be honest in everything that I do.

Amen

Israel's First King

1 Samuel 9:3

● ●

The people of Israel did not have a king. They told the prophet Samuel they wanted someone to lead them and help them fight their enemies. Samuel prayed to God and asked for help. God answered Samuel's prayer. God chose a man named Saul to be Israel's first king.

Saul's family owned many donkeys. One day, some of their donkeys ran away. Saul and a servant traveled to many places looking for the donkeys. But they could not find the lost donkeys anywhere.

In one town, the servant remembered that a prophet lived nearby. The servant told Saul about the prophet, whose name was Samuel. The prophet was very smart and might help them find the donkeys.

At that same time, God told Samuel that he was

going to meet a man. This man was going to be Israel's first king.

Samuel met Saul just as God had promised. Samuel told Saul that his donkeys had been found. Samuel poured special oil on Saul's head. Saul was surprised to hear that he was going to be Israel's first king.

Dear God,

What will I be when I grow up? You already know. But it will be an adventure for me to find out. Thank you for watching over me. Thank you for helping me in school. I pray that I will always be a good student.

Amen

Samuel Anoints David

1 Samuel 16:1

● ●

God had chosen Saul to be the first king of Israel. At first, Saul loved God and obeyed him. He was a wise and strong king. With God's help, Saul's armies defeated many of their enemies.

But then Saul began to disobey God. The prophet Samuel told Saul that he must follow God's rules. But Saul continued to turn away from God. Finally, God decided to choose a new king for Israel.

God sent Samuel to the town of Bethlehem. He would find a man named Jesse. One of Jesse's sons was going to be the next king of Israel.

Samuel met Jesse. Then Samuel met each son, one by one. They were tall, handsome men. Samuel thought that God would choose one of them to be Israel's next king. But God did not choose them.

Samuel asked Jesse if he had any more sons. Jesse told him that he had a young son named David. He was in the field caring for the family's sheep. Samuel asked to see David.

When David arrived, God told Samuel that David would be the next king. Samuel poured special holy oil on David's head, and God blessed him.

Dear God,

It's so interesting to hear stories about how you have worked in other people's lives. You don't always choose the oldest or the wisest. You chose little David, who just took care of his family's sheep. I pray that you will use me, too!

Amen

David Escapes

1 Samuel 18:10-11

With God's help, David defeated the giant soldier, Goliath, with a stone and a slingshot. By killing Goliath, David saved Israel's army. This pleased Israel's King Saul. So the king made David a leader in his army. Saul even invited David to live with him at his palace.

David was happy at the palace. Sometimes, he played his lyre for King Saul. Later, David married Saul's daughter, Michal.

David became a great leader in the king's army. He was a hero to the people of Israel. When he walked through the streets, they praised him. King Saul became jealous of David. He was afraid that David would soon try to take over his kingdom.

One day, David went to see King Saul. Suddenly the

king threw a spear at David and tried to kill him. David ran from the palace and went home to his wife.

Michal knew that David would not be safe if he stayed with her. She helped him get away safely. That night, King Saul's soldiers came to David's home to look for him. But thanks to his loving wife, David had already escaped.

Dear God,

I never want to be jealous of my friends. I want to be happy when good things happen to them. I want to be the first to cheer them on. I pray that you will help me to be a good and loyal friend.

Amen

Solomon Chooses Wisdom

1 Kings 3:3

● ●

King David had ruled Israel for a long time. Now he was old and very sick. He sent for his son Solomon. David had chosen Solomon to be the next king of Israel. David gave Solomon advice on being a good king. David also told him that he must obey God. Then God would always watch over him.

Soon after that, David died and Solomon became king. One night, God spoke to Solomon in a dream. In the dream, God offered Solomon a gift. God would give him whatever he wanted most.

Solomon could have asked for gold or jewels. But Solomon did not want any of those things. He was very concerned that he would not be a great king like his father. So Solomon asked God to give him wisdom. God answered his prayer and made him a wise king.

One day, two women came to see Solomon. Both women claimed to be the mother of one baby. Solomon ordered one of his men to cut the baby in half for the women to share. The real mother told Solomon she would rather give up her child than to have him killed. Solomon knew that she was the real mother. He happily gave the child to her.

Dear God,

I'm glad that you have given gifts to all of your children. I'm glad that I can ask you for wisdom. I want to be as wise as King Solomon. I pray that I will always know the right thing to do. Thank you for answering my prayers.

Amen

Solomon Builds a Temple

1 Kings 5:5

● ●

With God's help, King David made Israel a powerful nation. The people of Israel loved God and obeyed him. They worshiped at a special tent called a tabernacle. But they did not have a temple made of stone and wood. So King David planned to build a beautiful temple in Jerusalem. People would come there to pray, sing, and worship.

But God wanted David's son, Solomon, to build the temple when he became king. As soon as Solomon became the king of Israel, he began work on the temple. Solomon chose the best workers he could find. He also ordered the finest building materials.

Workers called masons cut big blocks of stone for the temple's high walls. Workers called carpenters built the temple roof and the floor from sturdy wood. Workers

covered the temple doors with gold. The temple was also decorated with beautiful wooden carvings.

After many years, the temple was finished. Solomon and the people of Israel held a celebration that lasted many days. Finally, the people of Israel had a temple where they could gather and praise God.

Dear God,

Wow! Building the temple was a really big job. When people love you, you are able to help them do their very best. I want to help build my place of worship, too. I can do that by giving my time to help my leaders. I pray that I will be a big help to them.

Amen

A Queen Visits Solomon

1 Kings 10:1

● ●

God blessed Solomon with great wisdom. Wise King Solomon helped his people with their problems. Soon people from faraway places traveled to see King Solomon for advice.

The queen of Sheba also heard about the wise king of Israel. She wanted to find out if what she had heard was true. So she made the long journey to Israel with her camels and her servants.

The king kindly welcomed the queen when she arrived at his palace. The queen asked King Solomon many hard questions. But the wise king answered each of her questions.

Then King Solomon had a great feast prepared for her. He showed her the beautiful palace and the temple he had built to worship God. She also saw that

his family and servants were very happy.

The queen now believed that Solomon was a wise and kind ruler. The queen offered Solomon gifts from her homeland. She brought him stacks of gold, spices, and beautiful jewels.

King Solomon gave her many precious gifts, too. Then the queen returned home with her gifts.

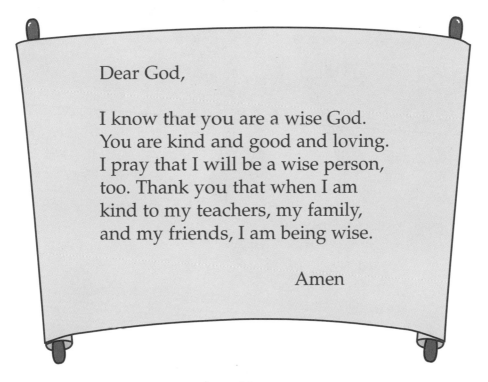

Dear God,

I know that you are a wise God.
You are kind and good and loving.
I pray that I will be a wise person,
too. Thank you that when I am
kind to my teachers, my family,
and my friends, I am being wise.

Amen

Elijah Is Fed

1 Kings 17:1

● ●

Long after King Solomon died, a new king ruled over Israel. King Ahab and his wife did not love God. The people of Israel forgot about God, too. They all believed in a false god. This made God very angry.

The prophet Elijah still worshiped God. He went to the palace and told the king that God was going to punish Israel. God would not allow any rain to fall for a long time.

When Elijah left the palace, God led him to the wilderness to hide from the king. God watched over Elijah. Each day, ravens brought him meat and bread. He drank water from a nearby stream.

Then God led Elijah to a city. God told him that he would meet a woman who would give him food. Elijah saw a woman gathering sticks near the city walls. Elijah

asked the woman for some food. But the woman was poor. She had only a little flour and some oil.

Elijah told the woman to go home. She would find enough flour and oil to last for a very long time. The woman went home and was amazed at what she saw. There was more than enough flour and oil for her and her son and Elijah.

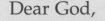

Dear God,

Help me always remember who you are. Remind me of all the good things you have done for me. Teach me to honor you every day. I know that when I obey you, you will reward me for my obedience.

Amen

Elisha Saves a Boy

2 Kings 4:18-19

● ●

Whenever the prophet Elisha traveled to the city of Shunem, he stayed with two of his friends. The rich woman and her husband even built a room for him on the top of their house. During one visit, Elisha announced that the couple would have a son. With God's help, the woman had a baby boy, just as Elisha had promised.

Many years passed. The man was working in the field one day. His son went to the field to see him. Suddenly, the boy told his father that his head was hurting. One of their helpers grabbed the boy and carried him home to his mother. But the boy died a short time later.

The woman carried her son to Elisha's room and laid him on Elisha's bed. Then she left quickly to find Elisha. She finally found Elisha and told him what had

happened. Elisha followed her back to her home.

Elisha went into the room with the boy and closed the door. Elisha asked God for help. God answered Elisha's prayer. The boy opened his eyes. God brought the boy back to life! It was a miracle! Elisha called for the woman. She ran into the room and held her son. Then she thanked Elisha for his help.

Dear God,

You have done so many amazing things! When I am sick, you are with me. When I am in danger, you are with me. Teach me to have the kind of faith that Elisha did. I pray that the first thing I do when I need help is to ask you for it.

Amen

Josiah and the Lost Scrolls

2 Kings 22:2

● ●

King Amon ruled over the Israelites. He did not worship God. He believed in false gods. Many Israelites believed in false gods, too.

When King Amon died, his young son, Josiah, became the king. Josiah worshiped God. He wanted his people to worship God, too.

Josiah decided that the temple in Jerusalem needed repairs. He chose workers to clean up the temple and make it beautiful again.

The workers started fixing the temple right away. One day, the high priest was walking through the temple. He found a scroll hidden in the corner. The scroll had some of God's laws written on it. He had never seen these laws before. The high priest ran to the palace and showed the scroll to the king's helper.

The helper read the scroll to King Josiah. The king ordered all the people to come to the temple. He read the scroll to them. Josiah and his people promised to worship God and obey his laws.

They had a great celebration to praise God. Then Josiah had all the statues of false gods knocked down and destroyed.

Dear God,

How easily the people of Israel forgot about you! I always want to remember that you are my God. I want to know your laws. I want to worship and praise you forever. I pray that you will bring teachers into my life to help me.

Amen

Esther Helps Her People

Esther 2:17

●●●●●●●●●●●●●●●●●●●●●●●●●●●●●

The king of Persia was looking for someone to become his queen. The king's helpers brought many women to the palace to meet the king. The king met some of the most beautiful women in the kingdom. But he was not pleased with any of them.

Then a young Jewish woman named Esther came to the palace to meet the king. She was beautiful and very wise. The king married Esther and made her the queen over his kingdom.

Haman, the king's best helper, ordered all Jewish people to bow down to him. But Esther's cousin Mordecai refused to bow to him. So Haman tricked the king into passing a new law. This law would allow Haman to get rid of all Jewish people in the kingdom.

When Esther heard about the new law, she went to

see the king. She told him that she was Jewish. Esther begged him not to harm her people. The king was very angry because Haman had tricked him.

The king changed the law. Brave Queen Esther saved her people. Then the king had Haman arrested for tricking him. Mordecai became his new helper.

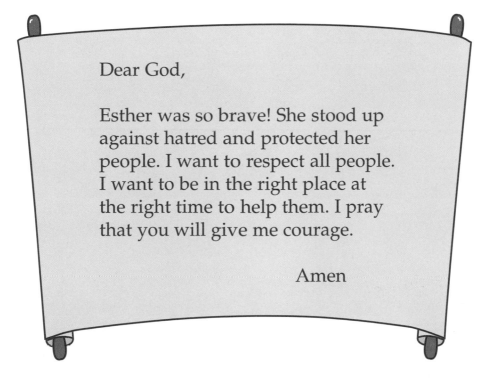

Dear God,

Esther was so brave! She stood up against hatred and protected her people. I want to respect all people. I want to be in the right place at the right time to help them. I pray that you will give me courage.

Amen

Faithful Job

Job 1:1

● ●

Job loved God very much. He was a very rich man. He had a beautiful home and a large family. He owned many animals and lots of land. Job was a very happy man.

Satan wanted to find out if Job would still love God if everything was taken from him. So Satan started taking things away from Job. First, one of Job's servants gave him some bad news. Some bad people had stolen many of his animals. They also killed most of his helpers. But Job still loved God.

Then Job received more bad news. Someone took the rest of his animals. A terrible storm killed most of his children. Satan made sure that Job lost everything. Finally, Satan put sores on Job's body. But Job did not blame God for his troubles.

Job's friends lied to him. They told him that God had caused all of his problems. But Job did not believe them. He asked God for help.

God gave Job more animals than he had before. God healed Job's sores. Job and his wife had ten more children. Then God blessed Job with a very long and happy life.

Dear God,

Why do people blame you when bad things happen to them? You are a good God. I know that you love me. I know that you want only the best for me. I pray that you will always protect me.

Amen

Daniel in the Lions' Den

Daniel 6:3

● ●

King Darius ruled over a large kingdom. He chose Daniel to be his best helper. The king's other helpers were jealous of Daniel. So they decided to get rid of him.

They spied on Daniel and saw him praying to God every day. They came up with a plan. The helpers tricked the king into passing a new law. This law said that all people must pray to the king. No one would be allowed to pray to God. Anyone who broke the law would be punished.

Daniel disobeyed the new law. He prayed to God anyway. The king liked Daniel, but he had to obey the law. So the king had Daniel thrown into the lions' den.

While Daniel was in the lions' den, the king worried about him. The next morning, the king went to see if

Daniel was all right. God had sent an angel to watch over Daniel and keep the lions' mouths shut.

The king was amazed that Daniel had not been harmed. He had Daniel freed from the lions' den. The king realized that God had saved Daniel. He changed the law and told everyone to worship God.

Dear God,

Laws are made to protect me. But a law that would forbid me from praying to you would be a bad law. I'm glad that I can pray to you any time I want to. I know that you hear my prayers. Teach me how to talk to you every day.

Amen

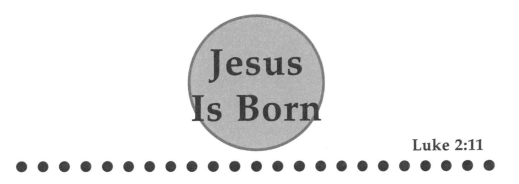

Jesus Is Born

Luke 2:11

● ●

A woman named Mary was happy that God had chosen her to give birth to his son. Her baby would be born very soon. But Mary and Joseph had to travel to the town of Bethlehem.

When they arrived in Bethlehem, Mary needed a place to rest. They searched for a place to stay. But all the inns were full. One innkeeper allowed them to spend the night in the stable with all the animals.

That night, baby Jesus was born. Mary gently wrapped up her baby to keep him warm. Then she laid him in a manger to sleep.

God sent angels to tell people about the birth of his son. One of the angels appeared to shepherds who were watching their sheep. The shepherds were frightened. But the angel told them not to be afraid. The angel gave

them good news. God's son had just been born in Bethlehem. Suddenly, the sky was filled with angels. They sang praises to God.

The shepherds went right away to visit the baby. They met Mary, Joseph, and baby Jesus. The shepherds praised God for letting them see this special baby. Then they returned to the fields.

Dear God,

What a wonderful night when Jesus was born! Because he was once a little child, he knows how it feels to be a kid. I love you, Jesus. I know you love me, too. Help me to show your love to others.

Amen

Three Wise Men

Matthew 2:1-2

● ●

Soon after Jesus was born, God placed a big star in the sky. It was bigger and brighter than all the other stars. One night, three wise men were looking at the sky. They noticed the bright star. The wise men believed this was a sign that a new king had been born. They left right away with gifts to offer the baby king.

The wise men followed the star as it moved through the sky. But before they could find the baby, King Herod sent for them. He had heard about the baby king, too. Herod was afraid the baby would try to take his place someday. So Herod planned to get rid of him.

The wise men went to see King Herod at his palace. He told them to return to the palace after they found the baby king.

They followed the star again. Finally, the star led

them to the town of Bethlehem. It stopped above the place where Jesus was staying with Mary and Joseph.

The wise men were happy to meet Jesus. They gave him gifts of gold and rare spices. Then they began their journey home. God warned them not to tell Herod where they had found baby Jesus. The wise men obeyed God and went straight home.

Dear God,

You led the wise men to baby Jesus with a bright star. Thank you that you lead me to him by your Spirit. I want to follow Jesus. I want to be like him. I pray that you will help me show Jesus' love to my family and friends.

Amen

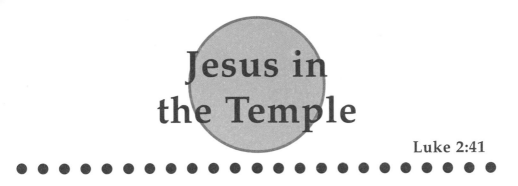

Jesus in the Temple

Luke 2:41

● ●

Every year, Mary and Joseph went to Jerusalem for Passover. They made the journey with many of their friends. The streets were crowded with people. They gathered at the temple to pray and worship God.

When Jesus was twelve years old, he went to the Passover festival with Mary and Joseph. When the festival was over, Mary and Joseph could not find Jesus in the crowd. But they believed that he was with some of their friends. So they began the long journey home.

As they traveled, Mary and Joseph asked their friends if they had seen Jesus. But nobody had seen him. Mary and Joseph were very upset. They returned to Jerusalem right away.

They went all over the city, looking for Jesus. They finally found him at the temple. Jesus was talking with

the priests at the temple. The priests were amazed that Jesus knew so much about God.

Mary and Joseph were happy to find Jesus. But Mary scolded Jesus for running away. Jesus knew that he was God's son. He told Mary that he was at the temple working for God, his father.

Dear God,

Mary and Joseph must have been very worried when they couldn't find Jesus. I know it's important that I always ask permission to go somewhere. I pray that I will always remember to tell someone where I am going.

Amen

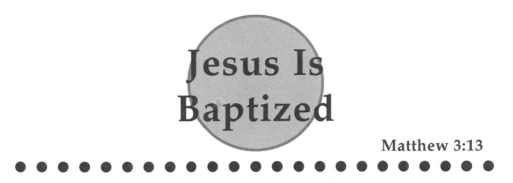

Jesus Is Baptized

● ●

John the Baptist lived in the wilderness. He wore clothes made from camel's hair and ate wild honey and locusts. God gave John the Baptist a very important job. He traveled to many places and talked to people about Jesus. He told them that Jesus is God's son. Jesus could forgive them for doing bad things.

Many people listened to John's words. They believed in Jesus. They were sorry that they had done bad things. John led them down to the river and baptized them. Then they were ready to live the way God wanted them to live.

One day, John the Baptist was preaching near the Jordan River. Jesus walked down to the river to see John. Jesus told John to baptize him.

John did not understand. He knew that Jesus was

perfect. Jesus did not need to be baptized. But John did as Jesus said. He led Jesus into the river and baptized him.

After Jesus was baptized, God sent a dove to fly in the sky. God said, "This is my Son, the Beloved, with whom I am well pleased."

Then Jesus traveled to the desert. He stayed there for many days to get ready to teach people about God's love.

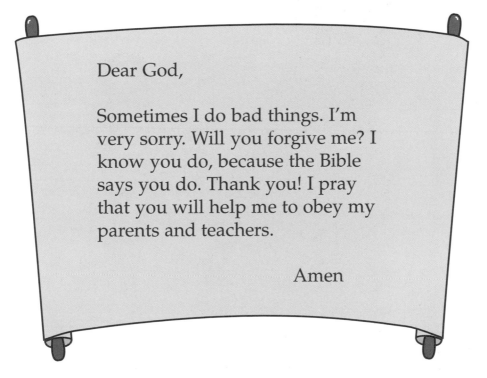

Dear God,

Sometimes I do bad things. I'm very sorry. Will you forgive me? I know you do, because the Bible says you do. Thank you! I pray that you will help me to obey my parents and teachers.

Amen

Jesus Chooses His Helpers

Matthew 4:18

● ●

Jesus was ready to teach people about God. But he knew he could not do it alone. He needed help to reach lots of people. He began to look for people to follow him. They would be his helpers and friends.

Jesus walked to a lake. He saw two fishermen. Peter and his brother Andrew were trying to catch fish with nets. Jesus told them to put down their nets and follow him. They were going to help him teach people about God. The two men quickly obeyed Jesus.

Later, Jesus met two more fishermen. James and his brother John were repairing a net. They left their nets behind and followed Jesus, too.

Then Jesus met a tax collector named Matthew. Tax collectors had the job of collecting money for the king. But most people did not like tax collectors because they

often took too much money. But Jesus knew that Matthew would be a good helper. So Matthew left his job and followed Jesus, too.

Jesus selected twelve men to be his helpers. They were called his disciples. Jesus taught them many things about God's love. They followed him and learned to trust him as God's son.

Dear God,

A job is so much easier to do when you have friends to help. Thank you for my friends. Thank you that we help each other. Teach me to follow you and trust you. I pray that you will show me how to be a better friend.

Amen

Jesus Heals a Servant

Matthew 8:5

● ●

News about Jesus spread quickly from town to town. Jesus and his disciples taught many people about God's love. Jesus performed many miracles. He healed people who had never been able to see. He cured people of terrible diseases.

Jesus and his disciples traveled to a city near the Sea of Galilee. The people there had already heard about Jesus' miracles. A huge crowd gathered to see him.

A Roman officer made his way through the crowd. The officer had a servant at his home whom he cared for very much. He told Jesus that his servant was very sick. His servant would die soon unless Jesus helped him.

Jesus offered to go to the officer's home right away and heal his servant. But the officer thought that he was not good enough to invite Jesus into his house. He

believed that Jesus could heal his servant just by saying the words.

Jesus was surprised by the officer's faith. He told the officer to go home. His servant would be healed. When the officer returned home, his servant was completely healed.

Jesus said to his disciples, "In no one in Israel have I found such faith."

Dear God,

I believe that Jesus healed many people. I believe he performed miracles, too. And I believe you love me just as much as you loved the servant. Thank you that you watch over me when I am sick. I pray that my faith will grow and grow.

Amen

Jesus Stops a Storm

Matthew 8:23-24

●●●●●●●●●●●●●●●●●●●●●●●●●●●

Jesus chose twelve men to be his disciples. They followed him everywhere. They ate with him and lived with him. The disciples watched him perform miracles. They helped him teach people about God.

After a short time together, Jesus taught his disciples many things. But they still did not understand that Jesus had the power of God to do great things.

Jesus and his disciples had been teaching a large group of people all day. They were very tired. They left the crowd and looked for a quiet place to rest. They climbed into a boat and sailed out on a nearby lake. Then Jesus fell asleep.

Suddenly a terrible storm came. The winds pushed big waves over the boat. The disciples were afraid that the boat was going to sink.

They woke Jesus and shouted, "Lord, save us!"
Jesus said, "Why are you afraid, you of little faith?"
He stood up and said, "Peace! Be still!"

The storm stopped. The disciples were amazed that Jesus had the power to change the weather. Jesus told them that they should always trust him to care for them and keep them safe.

Dear God,

I know that you care for me and keep me safe. I know that Jesus is my friend. I will remember that you are watching over me during a big storm. I pray that I will not be afraid of the wind and the rain.

Amen

The Story of
the Prodigal Son

Luke 15:11

Jesus often told stories called *parables* to help people understand God's love. Jesus told one story about a young man who lived with his father and his brother.

One day, the young man asked his father for some money. He wanted to travel and see the world. The young man's father gave him the money for his trip.

The young man spent lots of money on fancy clothes and fine food. Soon all the money was gone. The young man had to get a job feeding pigs. He was very sad.

The young man missed his family very much. But he was ashamed because he wasted all his money. The young man returned home. He told his father he was sorry for what he had done. The young man asked his father to give him a job as a servant.

The father was happy that his son had returned home safely. He forgave his son for spending all his money. He hugged and kissed his son. He even gave his son a big party to welcome him home.

Jesus was saying that God is like a loving earthly father. He always loves us. When we are sorry for doing bad things, he always forgives us.

Dear God,

You tell such wonderful stories in the Bible! Sometimes, I've wasted my money, too. But you forgive me when I do bad things. You love me no matter what. I pray that I will always remember that you are a loving father.

Amen

Jesus Meets Zacchaeus

Luke 19:1-2

● ●

Jesus was passing through the city of Jericho. A crowd of people gathered to meet him. There was a small man named Zacchaeus in the crowd. He wanted to see Jesus, too. But he could not see over the other people.

So Zacchaeus climbed a sycamore tree. He sat in the tree and watched Jesus talking to the other people. Then Jesus saw Zacchaeus sitting in the tree.

Jesus said, "Zacchaeus, hurry and come down; I must stay at your house today."

Zacchaeus was happy that Jesus was going to visit with him at his house. The people of Jericho did not like Zacchaeus. He made lots of money as a tax collector. He collected their money and gave it to the king. But Zacchaeus cheated the people. Sometimes he

took too much money for taxes. Then he kept the extra money that he collected.

Zacchaeus told Jesus that he was sorry for cheating the people. He promised to pay back all the extra money he took. Zacchaeus also promised to give lots of money to needy people. Jesus blessed Zacchaeus and forgave him for doing bad things.

Dear God,

I know that it's wrong to lie and cheat and steal. When I'm tempted to cheat in school, I will remember that you don't like cheating. I pray that you will help me to always be honest and tell the truth.

Amen

The People Welcome Jesus

Matthew 21:9

Jesus and his disciples were on their way to Jerusalem. They stopped at a hill near the city. Jesus told two of his disciples to go to a village nearby. They would find a donkey in the village. Jesus told them to bring the donkey to him.

The two disciples obeyed Jesus. They walked to the village and found the donkey just as Jesus had said. They took the donkey to Jesus.

Jesus climbed onto the donkey and rode it to Jerusalem. His disciples followed him. The streets of Jerusalem were crowded with visitors. They had gathered there to celebrate the Passover festival.

The people were very happy to see Jesus. They walked ahead of him and praised him. Many people placed palm leaves in the street as Jesus passed by.

They shouted, "Blessed is the one who comes in the name of the Lord!"

Jesus went to the temple to worship God. But the temple was filled with merchants. Jesus chased them from the temple. Then people who were very sick arrived at the temple to see Jesus. He healed them all.

Dear God,

It would have been exciting to see Jesus ride into Jerusalem on a donkey! I would have been happy to see Jesus, too. But I know that he is always with me, even when I can't see him. I pray that Jesus will live in my heart forever.

Amen

Jesus Goes to Heaven

Matthew 28:1

● ●

Jesus had many friends and followers. But some people did not believe that Jesus is God's son. They had him arrested and placed on a cross. After Jesus died on the cross, his friends buried his body in a tomb. They closed the tomb with a big stone.

Then Jesus came back to life just as he had promised. One day, Mary Magdalene and another woman went to the tomb. The stone had been rolled away, and Jesus was gone. An angel was inside the tomb. The angel told them that Jesus was alive again.

The women ran from the tomb to tell the disciples the good news. But Jesus met them on the way. The women were very happy to see Jesus. They bowed down at his feet. Jesus told them to get up and tell the disciples that he had risen from the dead.

Jesus spent many days talking to his disciples and many of his followers. Finally he led his disciples to a quiet place. He told them that God would watch over them. God would give them courage to continue preaching to others.

Jesus blessed each disciple. Then he went up to heaven in a cloud. They went to the temple and praised God.

Dear God,

It makes me sad to think about Jesus dying on a cross. But I know he did it for me. He did it so that I could live forever in heaven with you. How happy it makes me to know that he rose from the dead! I pray that I will always remember what Jesus did for me.

Amen

Saul Becomes Paul

Acts 9:4-5

Saul hated the people who worshiped Jesus. He had many of them arrested and thrown into prison. One day, Saul was walking to Damascus with some of his friends. A bright light filled the sky. Saul was frightened by the light and fell to the ground.

Saul heard someone speak to him. It was the voice of Jesus. Jesus told Saul to stand up and go to Damascus. But when Saul opened his eyes, he couldn't see. Saul's friends helped him reach Damascus.

Ananias was one of Jesus' followers in Damascus. He heard Jesus' voice, too. Jesus told him what had happened to Saul. He also told Ananias to find Saul in a house nearby. Ananias was afraid. He knew that Saul hated Jesus' followers. But Ananias obeyed Jesus. He found Saul just as Jesus had told him.

Ananias placed his hands on Saul and said, "The Lord Jesus . . . has sent me so that you may regain your sight and be filled with the Holy Spirit."

Suddenly, Saul could see again. He asked God to forgive him for all the bad things he had done. Later Saul changed his name to Paul. He spent the rest of his life teaching people about Jesus.

Dear God,

This story shows that even bad people can change. Saul hated Jesus' friends, but when he met Jesus, he totally changed. I know that I'm not perfect, either. Sometimes, I do bad things, too. But I pray that you will help me to change.

Amen

Paul Spreads the Word

Acts 13:1

● ●

Before he believed in Jesus' teachings, Paul hated Jesus' followers. Now he was teaching people to follow Jesus. He helped start a church so that people could worship together.

While Paul and others were worshiping at their church, God spoke to them. God told them to send Paul and his friend Barnabas on a long journey.

Paul and Barnabas traveled to many cities. They taught many people about Jesus. God even gave Paul the power to heal people. In one city, Paul met a man who had never been able to walk. Paul told him to stand up. The man instantly stood up and walked!

Some people did not believe what the two men told them. They even tried to kill Paul and Barnabas. But God watched over them. Paul and Barnabas did not give up. With God's help, they started new churches where

people learned about Jesus' teachings.

Later Paul made two more journeys. Paul and his friends continued to start new churches. They also visited churches that they had already started. Paul and his friends were arrested many times. But Paul continued to spread Jesus' teachings. He even wrote parts of the Bible, with God's help.

Dear God,

Thank you that, because of people like Paul, I know about Jesus. I want to tell others about all the wonderful things Jesus did, too. I can do it with your help. I pray that I will have the courage to tell my friends and family about the love of Jesus.

Amen

If you have enjoyed this book or if it has impacted your life, we would like to hear from you. Please contact us at:

Honor Books
Department E
P. O. Box 55388
Tulsa, Oklahoma 74155

Or by e-mail at info@honorbooks.com

Additional copies of this book and other Honor Books titles are available from your local bookstore.